MIND YOUR GOAL POST

BY

DANNY GEORGE AWAIKO

LEGAL DISCLAIMER

Published in Nigeria by
DANGOFE PUBLISHING HOUSE
3 Duenta Street, Abuloma,
Port-Harcourt, Rivers State, Nigeria.
TEL: +23408063689774, +23408056738866
Email: dannygeorge002@yahoo.com

ISBN: 9798714348259

TABLE OF CONTENT

Danny George Awaiko

Dedication

This book is dedicated to Juanita my daughter.

Chapter One

Everyone has a goal post

Every goal keeper in a football match has his own goal post. The more he minds his goal post the better he becomes at what he is doing. Every goal keeper in a football match stops the ball from entering his own net. You see him organizing his defenders to make sure he is not exposed to any shot from their opponents, so that they might not concede any goal. Every good goal keeper will never leave his goal post or line and start playing the role of a defender, midfielder or attacker. If he does, in most cases he might concede a cheap goal.

Furthermore, in every football match we always have two goal keepers minding their individual goal post. It will be ironical if goal keeper "A" decides to leave his own goal post to go and assist goal keeper "B" in his own goal post. His own goal post will not only be exposed but his team will concede plenty of goals. He might be sacked from that club because of his incompetence and be replaced by another goal keeper who is ready to mind his own goal post.

In real life every man has his own goal post. Are you a Lawyer, Doctor, Teacher, Pastor, Banker, Business man, Journalist, Politician etc. you have a goal post. So many persons in life have lost focus, because they left their own goal post. The day you leave your goal line you will start malfunctioning. Many persons are sitting in the middle of nowhere because they left their goal post. It is so dis-heartening and sad, that most persons in life move from one goal post to another without achieving anything.

As an individual, I know my area of specialty, so I don't have any business to envy or try to be like another person. For the fact that your friend is making impact in his own field does not mean you cannot make impact with what you are known for. When you leave your goal post as the goal keeper of a small club in England for a bigger club, of course you know you will malfunction because that is not your goal post. You need time to get to that level. That does not mean you are not relevant in your small club, which small club is your goal post for now and you have to be serious about it. Vying for the position to become the American president is not for every person. Everyone has his own area of specialty. John the Baptized in the bible was not the messiah but mind his goal post by preparing the way for the messiah. You must not be the head of an organization or a team leader, before you can make impact. Minding your goal post is the best thing that can happen to you. Leaving your goal post to go and test another person's goal post to know if it fits you; might be a big risk, because by the time you return someone else has taken over your goal post. Even when you struggle to fit in, you will discover at the end of the day that you are irrelevant.

A young man named Peter who come sunshine or rain will be at the train station distributing gospel tracts to passengers as they board or leave the train. This he did severally for several years.

One day at the church service after a song rendition by the choir members in church, the church members praised and gave a standing ovation. Peter instead of being happy for them was very sad. He thought his soul winning effort was not being acknowledged, rewarded or recognized by the church ministers or members. He also noticed that nobody from the station has met him to say thank you for what he has been faithfully doing all these years. So he decided to abandon the trips to the Train station. Instead he left his goal post and joined the choir and started singing with them. To his surprise he was warmly welcomed. He discovered also that very soon he was singing and receiving standing ovations. He concluded in his mind he has just made the right decision.

One day he sang psalm 23 as a soloist and by the time he finished singing the whole church including the pastoral team, the elders were on their feet clapping and giving him a standing ovation.

Suddenly, there arose an old man, a stranger in the midst of the congregation who was asked to sing the same song while the church was still on their feet clapping for the soloist. Against protocol the pastor cynically allowed the old man to sing. By the time the old man finished singing the whole church was on their knees, some weeping others praying in repentance. That day there were no more sermons but an altar call with sinners giving their lives and backsliders returning to their first love? The whole church rededicated their lives to God.

This young man who left his goal post at the train station became devastated. He felt empty. He saw the difference between when men are appreciating you, and when God is appreciating you for what you are doing.

He left the choir with a heavy heart without thinking of removing his choir robe; he headed for the Train station the goal post he left. On getting there he met a man in the same spot where he used to stand to distribute gospel leaflets before. The man was distributing gospel tracts and handed him one.

With tears in his eyes he asked the man how he came to start distributing the tracts at the Train Station. The busy man not looking at him told him of a dead man who used to come there come sunshine and rain to distribute tracts. That for months the man has not been there. He told him he believe and concluded the man must be dead. He said the dead man gave him a tract before that changed his commitment to Christ. So he decided to take his position to continue the good work of what he has been doing.

What a sympathetic story, this young man left his goal post where he was affecting lives for another man's goal post because he lost focus. On returning back his goal post has been occupied by another man.

This story is a replica of what happens every day to great minds of men and women, who leave there goal post to another man's post. You don't need to pack your bags yet from that office, business, or church. For the fact that everybody is doing a particular thing, does not mean you must do that same thing.

Mind your goal post

Stay put to what you are doing. The sky will be your starting point.

Chapter Two

You are the best in your goal post

Every goal keeper in a football match believes he is the best. Your goal post represents your area of specialty. Are you a businessman, furniture maker, pastor, writer, journalist, teacher, lawyer etc. you are the best. As a writer I don't believe anybody writes better than me. I believe my write ups are the best. The reason why most persons are been humiliated in their field is because they don't believe they are the best. You must believe in yourself and speak positive things about what you do. For the fact that you are a lawyer and you have other senior lawyers around you, does not mean they are better than you. You are the best in your goal post. If you don't believe you are the best nobody will believe in you.

Mind your goal post

David in the bible believed he was the best in his goal post. That's why when he was been discouraged not to fight goliath he never adhere to it. He fought and defeated goliath and was crowned the new champion. You can be crowned the new champion in that area of endeavor.

A goal keeper in the same team with other goalkeepers will always tell you he is the best. Your body language will always portray the real you. Don't give room for low self –esteem; it will only give you a wrong picture of who you are. I have been to so many places where I was almost intimidated by the presence of persons around, but I keep telling myself I am the best. Just mind your goal post and be confident in what you are doing.

Take a look at the world of football, two persons, Messy and Ronaldo; have ruled the world of football for a decade because they believe they are the best in the world of football. Messy has won the FIFA player award in 2009,2010,2011,2012 and 2015. Ronaldo has won it for 2008, 2013, 2014, 2016, and 2017.

Why the two? Are there no other footballers? Your response is as good as mine.

Fusain St Leo Bolt is another man who believes he is the best. Born 21st August 1986, is a Jamaican retired sprinter and world record holder in the 100 meters, 200 meters, and 4x100 meters relay. His reign as Olympic Games champion in all these events spans three Olympics. Due to his achievements and dominance in sprint competition, he is widely considered to be the greatest sprinter of all time. My question is, are there no other sprinters in the world? Why him? He believes he is the best in his goal post.

You can be the best doctor among doctors, pastor among pastors, banker among bankers, teacher among teachers, business man among business men, etc. if only you can prove to the world that you are the best. Just look at the mirror and tell yourself the truth, that you are the best in your goal post.

Your gloves is unique, is the focus of the next chapter.

Chapter Three
Your Gloves Is Unique

I have overheard so many goalkeepers in a football match who complained that the reason why they did not perform well or why they conceded a goal in a football match was because of the kind of hand gloves they used. As a goalkeeper if you don't use the right gloves you might end up making mistakes. Can you imagine a goalkeeper using an oversized glove or an undersized gloves; he will never be comfortable with it. He might end up making careless mistakes that will make his team to lose the match.

For you to continue to mind your goal post effectively, you need the right gloves. One thing is to mind your goal post another thing is to use the right gloves. Your Glove in this context represents your ideas in the journey of life. For the fact that the ideas of the other person worked for him or her, does not mean it will work for you. You have to initiate your own ideas which might be the right gloves for you.

As far as I am concern your gloves is unique and cannot be compared with another person's gloves. The ideas the president of Canada will use to govern his country may not be a workable idea in Brazil, because the terrain in Canada is totally different from Brazil. Let me make it clear, I am not saying that emulating another person's idea is totally bad. However, I want you to know that there is this uniqueness when you brain storm and get your own ideas to solve situations.

However, we are not condemned to a particular outcome. The qualities that make every person a unique interesting individual can be honed, improved upon, and made to grow as we continue our life's journey. Here are just some of the things that make you unique in this world.

Your Personality

An individual's personality is something that is molded from the moment they are born right through to the present moment. No one else can or will have your exact collection of knowledge, experiences, and perceptions that causes you to be who you are. No one else is going to respond to what you've experienced with the same emotions and thoughts that you had. No one is going to make the same choices that you make. Your personality is uniquely your own.

Your attitude

A person's attitude dictates how they perceive life and the actions of the people around them. Both a positive and negative attitude can be infectious, influencing the people around you and pulling them in the general direction of what you are putting into the world.

Your Experiences

A person's past and future experiences have without a doubt the greatest influence on shaping who they are as a unique individual. Every experience helps us determine how we will end up interacting with the world and other people in it.

Your Habits

A habit is a thing we do with great regularity. The habits we have inform and determine what aspects of our unique person we develop.

Your creativity

Creativity is an interesting thing because there are so many different kinds. You have a variety of arts that flex creative side of your brain, from painting and drawing to dance and singing. But then you also have creativity in other forms, like developing efficient systems, building a bookcase with your own hands, or planning an aesthetically pleasing landscape. Every person has their own unique, creative gifts which are influenced by their own vision.

Your perspective

Can anyone in the world see the world exactly as you do? No one else has lived twenty-four hours a day, seven days a week, and three hundred and sixty-five days a year. No one else has experienced life in the same way that you have. No one else has the exact same body of knowledge that you have. A person's perspective is uniquely their own. That's why it's so important to be open to other people's opinions and ideas. Not necessarily to accept them as right or wrong, but to help fill in the blanks and continue to develop your unique perception of the world. An exchange of ideas with the right person on your perceptions of the world can unlock. Realization and wisdom so don't shy away from listening to or sharing your own perspectives and opinions.

Your taste

What do you like? What do you dislike? Though we can find common ground with other people on what constitutes quality or beauty. Your tastes are largely a unique facet of your personality. A person's taste will influence many of their choices in life, whether it's what food to eat or what type of people they want to have a relationship with.

Your Goals

A person's goals generally guide how they spend their time, energy, and effort. The areas of life and endeavors where we invest out time, energy, and effort are going to be the things we have in mind most often, which will influence what we give back and take from the world. Short, medium, and long-term goals provide us direction and motivation when we feel lost or like we are stumbling on our path.

Your hobbies

What do you like to do for fun? It's a common question that people use as an icebreaker, and it speaks to the type of person you are. Hobbies certainly don't define a person, but what you spend your time informs others about what kind of person you are. Do you like puzzles? Sports, Volunteer work, gardening, cooking, gaming, all of these things say something about you as a unique individual. Your values and how you seek happiness or meaning in life.

Your passion

Passion is a magnificent part of the human experience. There are so many things to be passionate about- art, nature, and humanity to name a few. Passions can provide much needed direction toward a goal or experience that will allow us to leave our own unique mark on the world. Understanding your passions can help you find direct, distinct path that is guided by your values and unique perception of the world. We are all unique individuals. We all have something unique and valuable to contribute to the world.

CHAPTER FOUR
WORK WITH A TEAM

Every goal keeper will always work with a team. For a goal keeper to succeed minding his goal post he must work with other ten players in the field to help him prevent goals from entering his goal post. You will always see the goal keeper shouting on his defenders, midfielders, and attackers to be organized most especially when a free kick is to be taken by their opponents. At the end of the day the ball will either be deflected or bounce back, do to good defending.

Just as the goal keeper in a football match works with his team mates to defend his goal post so also every man or woman in every facets of life must work with a team to succeed. Minding your goal post in life is good but minding your goal post without a team is ironical. So, if you are a Doctor you need to team up with other doctors to achieve distinction in your profession. As a pastor minding your goal post you need a team of other pastors to achieve your set objectives in ministry. Whatever position or facet of life you belong to, you need to work with a team.

What is team work?

Teamwork is the collaborative effort of a group to achieve a common goal or to complete a task in the most effective and efficient way. This concept is seen within the greater framework of a team, which is a group of interdependent individuals who work together towards a common goal.

How to work with a team

Be Respectful of Each Other

You're never going to agree with everyone in a team environment. However, it's important to be respectful of others' opinions and to recognize that in a group, there is not one single right way to approach a project. Raise legitimate questions or concerns, but don't belittle colleagues or call them out for what you consider to be bad ideas. Its majority rule in most team environments, so chances are if an idea is off base, others in the group will speak up as well.

Don't Be a Slacker

Even when specific roles and responsibilities are assigned to team members, there's going to be some overlap. Someone will work a little more and someone will work a little less than the others. While you shouldn't jump in to pick up every dropped ball on a project, make an effort to contribute at 100 percent, meet deadlines, and be willing to lend a hand to advance the team's initiatives when needed.

Don't Gossip About Others

Gossiping about team members only leads to a sense of distrust, which can potentially derail the good work you're trying to accomplish. If you have a problem with a team member, discuss it privately or involve your team leader. Don't segregate into smaller groups within the team. This action only fragments efforts and creates an uncomfortable and unproductive working environment.

Recognize the Contributions of Others

There's no "I" in team, but that doesn't mean members don't like to be singled out for their positive efforts and contributions. Acknowledge the work of others and express your appreciation for their creativity and insight. It infuses the team with enthusiasm and creates a sense of camaraderie that is valuable as you work collectively as a unit.

An environment of teamwork has the potential to produce exceptional results, as well as provide dynamic and interesting work experiences. Approach this type of opportunity with tact, diplomacy and professionalism to ensure optimal results.

About The Author

Danny George Awaiko is a young dynamic Revivalist, a Preacher, a Motivational Speaker, and a man who loves the Holy Spirit. He also shares his insight with singles. He is a self-publishing author, and has written several inspirational books like: sex without knowledge, The Secret Is Out, Checklist for savings and investment, 21 Ways to Identify False Prophets, 7 Catalyst of Revival, 24 Secrets of Worship, Holy Spirit My Best Friend and many others.

For 13 years he has impacted on so many youths in different higher institutions, which led to him winning the Aaron and Hur's award as his first award in 2008. His first book, "The Secret Is Out", has reached out to many lives. He is a mindset coach, a personal development speaker, and a financial analyst. Danny lives in Port-Harcourt, Nigeria and loves writing, reading, fitness and travelling.

Other Books By: Danny George Awaiko

1) The Secret Is Out

2) Destiny Plucked Out Of Fire.

3) Holy Spirit my best friend

4) 24 secrets of worship

5) 21 Ways to Identify False Prophets

6) 7 killing D'S OF Destiny

7) 7 Catalyst of Revival

8) 7 Spirits Militating Against the Church

9) 10 Steps to become a Champion.

10) Checklist for Savings and Investment

11) Sex without knowledge

12) The Myth about Sex

13) 21 reasons why you are hot and still single

14) How the Holy Spirit incubates you as a minister

15) Where is Judas Iscariot?

16) Intercessors without walls.

Connect With Me

Thank you for buying and reading this book, please remember to leave reviews and connect with me on social media platforms:

Email: dannygeorge002@yahoo.com

Facebook: @ dannygeorge

Twitter: @ dannygeorge

Mobile Number: +2348063689774

WATTSAPP: +2348158263438